A Little Book of
HEALING
PRAYER

ANGELA ASHWIN

GRAND RAPIDS, MICHIGAN 49530 USA

For Pat

who first encouraged me to write prayers

ZONDERVAN

A Little Book of Healing Prayer
Copyright © 1996 by Angela Ashwin

Requests for information should be addressed to:
Zondervan, *Grand Rapids, Michigan 49530*

Library of Congress Cataloging-in-Publication Data

Ashwin, Angela
    A little book of healing prayer / written and compiled by Angela
Ashwin.
        p. cm.
    Originally published: Great Britain : Marshall Pickering, 1996.
    Includes bibliographical references and index.
    ISBN 0-310-24949-X
    1. Prayers. 2. Healing – Prayer-books and devotions – English.
I. Title
BV260 .A84 2002
242'.8 – dc21   2002007259

This selection is taken from Angela Ashwin's anthology, *The Book of a
Thousand Prayers*, with a few additions.

All prayers are by Angela Ashwin unless otherwise stated.

Interior design by Todd Sprague

Printed in the United States of America

A Little Book of
HEALING
PRAYER

Also by Angela Ashwin:
The Book of a Thousand Prayers
A Little Book of Bible Promises
A Little Book of Daily Prayer
A Little Book of Women's Prayer
Prayer in the Shadows

CONTENTS

INTRODUCTION

All prayer is concerned with healing, in the widest sense of that word, because, whenever we pray, we open ourselves to receive the transforming love of God. Just as we cannot swim without getting wet, so we cannot pray without being touched by God, who responds to us at our point of need, and uses our prayers to bless others.

Healing, then, is concerned not only with backaches and bitterness, but also with work and relationships, communities and celebrations, local and international concerns. Intercession is always a healing activity, because in offering ourselves as channels of God's love to others we become more whole ourselves. Prayers of thanksgiving and stillness can also be profoundly healing experiences. When we are specifically asking God for physical healing, we need to see this kind of prayer in a wider context. Those who spend a lot of time with sick people say that bodily symptoms sometimes change when inner problems and old hurts are addressed and opened up to the light of God. Furthermore, prayer goes hand in hand with medical treatment, and is never meant to be a 'religious alternative' or a desperate last resort.

Inner healing can also take place when death is approaching. I have known people with terminal illnesses who discovered a new quality of life during their last months. In some cases, their awareness of God deepened; at the very time when they were facing up to their dying, their living was enriched, and many memories and relationships were healed.

Some people appear to think that praying for healing is a sort of bargaining-match with God, as if we could cajole him to act in the way we want as long as we can muster enough 'faith'. This is clearly nonsense. Healing is God's free gift, which he pours upon us in his own way and in his own time. We do not know how he will touch us. But, when we do expose our situations to him, we can be confident that he will be there with us and working in us.

In a sense we all need healing, for each of us is bruised, weary or hurt in some way; those of us who are physically fit stand alongside people who are ill in our common need of God's forgiveness and love.

USING THESE PRAYERS

The value of a small book like this is that it fits easily into a pocket or handbag. The prayers can be used at any time or place, even in queues, buses or station platforms. For particular needs and concerns there is an Index of Subjects. Or, if you wish, you can work systematically through the prayers, from beginning to end. The advantage of this approach is that it relieves you of the effort of having to plan or decide which prayers to use. You simply take what is given, make that your offering, and let God use it in whatever way he wants. Obviously some prayers are meant for specific circumstances. But, in general, going straight through the sections can become a useful part of a regular prayer-pattern, especially if you have a chance to be quiet after using a prayer.

I hope that this collection will enable readers to let go into God's love, and be healed by the same energy that flowed through Jesus whenever he encountered people. Fortunately the value of our praying does not depend on our own skill or worthiness. When we pray, Christ comes to meet us, praying in us and making good our imperfect efforts, so that we are taken up into his life and work in the world. Thus we are made whole.

Personal
Prayers

LORD, HEAL AND HELP ME

1

Here I am, Lord,
    wounded
    worried
divided against myself.
Here I am
    naked
    numb
    exposed to you.
Here I am
    held
    healed
    loved
passive in the arms of my God.

2

Lord, come as sweet, healing oil
into my weary mind,
my bruised heart
and my dried-up soul.

3

You meet me in gentleness.
You come close.
You take my coldness
and warm me from the inside.
As my cold heart melts, Lord,
let your streams flow through me,
that I may play my part
in the renewing of the earth.

Based on some words of Ulrich Schaffer

4

Lord,
I want to reach you
and I try to touch you,
but many forces jostle me
and my own fears thrust me aside.

I want to reach you
and I try to touch even your garment,
but they say I am a fool
and I am filled with doubt.

I want to reach you
and I try to touch even the hem of your garment,
and my fingers brush the homespun cloth
and I am flooded with healing
and you turn and ask who touched you
and I fall on my face
and you bend down, lifting me gently, and telling me
that my own faith, that fragment of hope,
has healed me.

And you love me,
and my life is changed.

The woman with a haemorrhage, Luke 8:43–48

5

Now my life is hidden with Christ in God;
I am yours, Lord,
for better, for worse,
in times of hope when I feel well and alive,
and in the bleak landscape of my darkness;
in it all
I am yours.

Colossians 3:3

6

Lord, cleanse and sweeten the springs of my being,
that your freedom and light
may flow into my conscious mind
and into my hidden, unconscious self.

7

Gentle God, ground of my beseeching,
you enfold me in goodness
and wrap me tenderly as in a garment;
be my true rest,
and make me one with you.

God my Father, my Mother, my Spouse,
let love be my meaning
as it is yours,
and keep me always
in the love with which you loved me
before I was born.

Based on teachings of Julian of Norwich (c. 1342–1413)

8

Lord,
through weariness and hurt,
through disaster on the news,
through headaches and depression,
I am still yours.
I do not understand,
but I believe that you are here
in the dark places of human life,
and that nothing
can take us out of your hands.

9

O God,
I am hurt
and I am wrestling:
wrestling with the self-pity that threatens to
    swallow me up;
wrestling with my reluctance to admit my own
    failings;
wrestling with loneliness and the longing to be
    fully understood.

Who am I wrestling with, God?
Myself?
The evil one?
Or is it with You,
my Guarding Angel,
my God,
who will not let me go,
until I rest
exhausted but healing
in Your arms,
as Your sorrow dissolves my pride,
and Your love penetrates my scars?

Jacob wrestles with God, Genesis 32:24–32

10

I will face this pain.
I will accept its full impact
silently
turning my gaze
onto the crucified Christ
who is in this hell with me.
Even here
I am held in the love of Jesus
who is both Love-in-death
and Love-Risen.

11

Lord,
I am tearing the heart of my soul in two.
I need you to come
and lie there yourself
in the wounds of my soul.

Mechtild of Magdeburg (1207–1294)

12

Holy Spirit of God,
baptise me with your grace
like early morning dew.
Divine Comforter,
heal my wounds,
and soothe and quieten my mind
with your message of peace.

13

Lord Jesus Christ, who stopped to listen
to blind Bartimaeus in his frustration,
look also on me
with your eyes of love.
Restore my inward sight,
renew my sense of self-worth,
and take hold of my hands
as I join you on the way.

Mark 10:46–52

14

anoint the wounds
of my spirit
with the balm
of forgiveness
pour the oil
of your calm
upon the waters
of my heart

take the squeal
of frustration
from the wheels
of my passion
that the power
of your tenderness
may smooth
the way I love

that the tedium
of giving
in the risk
of surrender
and the reaching
out naked
to a world
that must wound

may be kindled
fresh daily
to a blaze
of compassion
that the grain
may fall gladly
to burst in the ground
– and the harvest abound.

Ralph Wright O.S.B.

15

Jesus, as a mother you gather your people to you:
you are gentle with us like a mother with her
children.

Often you weep over our sins and our pride: tenderly you draw us from hatred and judgement.

You comfort us in sorrow and bind up our
wounds: in sickness you nurse us and with pure
milk you feed us.

Jesus by your dying we are born to new life: by
your anguish and labour we come forth in joy.

Despair turns to hope through your sweet goodness: through your gentleness we find comfort in
fear.

Your warmth gives life to the dead: your touch
makes sinners righteous.

In your compassion bring grace and forgiveness:
for the beauty of heaven may your love prepare us.

Jesus, in your love and tenderness, remake us.

Saint Anselm (1033–1109)

16

Lord, life is empty, miserable and dreary;
free me from this self-imprisonment.
I feel worthless, yet I do matter to you.
You love me.
Help me to find freedom in that.

I am heavy and lifeless,
in the darkness with you –
yet you are more than darkness.

This depression is like a huge wave:
help me to ride on it
rather than being engulfed by it.
No matter how awful I feel,
remind me that you are always loving me.
This is hard work, God.
Much easier to slump back
into a cushion of misery.
Give me strength
for the effort of each moment as it comes –
for this moment.

DURING ILLNESS

17

Lord, hang on to me, because I don't feel
well enough to hang on to you.

18

Lord, this is unbearable. Even though I'm grateful
for all the help from people rallying round, I hate
the fact that I need them. Help me to receive as
well as to give. Teach me to use this illness posi-
tively, as a chance to let go of my desire always to
be organized, competent and in control. Set my
spirit free – I know I am valuable to you, even
when I'm stuck here!

19

Take, Lord, my heart, my life,
a vessel broken by ill-health,
shattered by loss,
emptied of ambitions and strivings.

Fill it with your love,
your joy, your grace, so full
that out of the cracks of pain,
the gashes of frustration,
the holes of despair,
may seep,
cleansing those wounds,
hope, comfort, healing,
to those for whom I pray,
and those you love, beyond my prayers.

Anne Lepine

WHEN BUSY AND OVER-TIRED

20

Even if my old and familiar ways of praying are
    taken away from me,
I am never taken away from you, Lord,
for you are here, reaching out to me,
loving me now.

Even when I am denied a space to be quiet with you,
there is still space inside me, Lord,

an inner room where you are waiting for me,
and which I can enter at any moment.

Even though I feel miserable and worthless,
I am still precious in your eyes
because I am your child,
and you are waiting to open your arms and
      embrace me.

21

Lord, grant me strength to do what has to be
      done today,
and wisdom calmly to leave on one side what
      cannot be done.
Fill me with prayer,
draw together my scattered preoccupations,
and help me to respond to every moment with my
      full attention;
for your love's sake.

22

Lord, when I am feeling tired and strained, help
me not to take it out on other people.

23

Lord, you put twenty-four hours in a day, and
gave me a body which gets tired and can only do
so much. Show me which tasks you want me to
do, and sharpen my senses, that I may truly
    see what I am looking at,
    taste what I am eating,
    listen to what I am hearing,
    face what I am suffering,
    celebrate the ways I am loved,
    and offer to you whatever I am doing,
so that the water of the present moment
    may be turned into wine.

DIFFICULT RELATIONSHIPS

24

Lord, pick me up and put me together again.
Sometimes things become unbearable, and
being with *N.* brings out the worst in me.
Help me. Forgive my resentment and sharp
reactions. Free me from endless churning over

arguments in my mind. Stay at my centre,
Lord, and let nothing take from me that inner
point of sanity, where I am known by you and
not condemned.

25

Lord, this is what went wrong . . .
I give it all to you, every detail, every barb, every
    frustration,
the major things and the petty things.
May the pain which I am feeling be for healing,
    and not a spring of bitterness.
May my hurts be Christ-centred, and for those
    involved,
rather than self-centred and against them.

IN BEREAVEMENT

26

My God,
why have you let this happen?

why did you forsake us?
Creator – why uncreate?
Redeemer – why destroy wholeness?
Source of love – why rip away
the one I loved so utterly?
Why? Why, O God?

In this pit of darkness,
hollowed out by grief and screaming,
I reach out to the one I loved
and cannot touch.

Where are you, God?
Where are you,
except here
in my wounds
which are also yours?

God,
as I hurl at you
my aching rage and bitterness,
hold me,

and stay here
until this hacked-off stump of my life
discovers greenness again.

27

O God who brought us to birth,
and in whose arms we die:
in our grief and shock contain and comfort us;
embrace us with your love,
give us hope in our confusion,
and grace to let go into new life,
through Jesus Christ.

Janet Morley

LORD, FORGIVE ME

28

Lord Jesus,
forgive me for failing you,
as even the first disciples did.
Through thoughtlessness
I betray you;
through fear
I run away from you;
through cowardice
I deny you,
not wanting people to know that I am a follower
of yours.
Have mercy on me,
as you had mercy on Peter and the others,
and, when the cock crows in my heart,
and I realize what I have done,
help me to bear your gaze of love.

29

I open my eyes, O God, to the glory and sunshine
      in your creation,
and I open my heart to receive the full impact of
      your love.
May your radiant fire burn away all that is rotten
      in me.
Let me breathe in the fresh air of life on which I
      depend in the miracle of existence.
May the wind of your Spirit blow through me and
      clear away the cobwebs and the rubbish.
I surrender my whole being to the wind and sun
      of your love.

30

How could I ever imagine
that I would cope without praying?
How could I keep going
unless I knew
that I could return my heart to you
and soak my darkness in your light?
Pour your mercy into my madness
and your Spirit into my will,

and make me know
in my heart as well as my head
that only in you
am I found, forgiven and free.

31

Love of Jesus, fill me,
Joy of Jesus, surprise me,
Peace of Jesus, flood me,
Light of Jesus, transform me,
Touch of Jesus, warm me,
Strength of Jesus, encourage me,
O Saviour, in your agony, forgive me,
in your wounds, hide me,
and in your risen life take me with you,
for your love's sake.

32

O blessed Jesus, give me stillness of soul in Thee.
Let Thy mighty calmness reign in me;
Rule me, O King of gentleness, King of peace.
Give me control, great power of self-control,

Control over my words, thoughts and actions.
From all irritability, want of meekness, want of
     gentleness,
Dear Lord, deliver me.
By Thine own deep patience, give me patience.
Make me in this and all things more and more
     like Thee.

Saint John of the Cross (1542–1591)

33

Lord, I am part of the tension and injustice of the
     world.
     Forgive our human selfishness, to which I con-
     tribute;
     heal the resentment between people, of which
     I am a part;
     and come into the world's conflicts, in which I
     share by being human.
Take my unworthiness and sorrow,
and use them in your great work
of healing and redeeming humanity.

34

Lord, what are my riches?
What stops me giving everything to you?
What weighs me down and ties my hands?
What denies me true freedom?
Show me,
and give me grace to abandon my idols,
so that, when you look at me with love,
I shall not walk away,
like the rich young man,
still cluttered.

The rich young man, Mark 10:17–22

35

Come, O Christ my Light, and illumine my
    darkness.
Come, my Life, and revive me from death.
Come, my Physician, and heal my wounds.
Come, Flame of divine love, and burn up the
    thorns of my sins,
kindling my heart with the flame of your love.
For you alone are my King and my Lord.

Saint Dimitrii of Rostov (17th century)

36

Save me, Lord, from the distraction
of trying to impress others,
and from the dangers of having done so.
Help me to enjoy praise for work well done,
and then to pass it on to you.
Teach me to learn from criticism,
and give me the wisdom
not to put myself at the centre of the universe.

37

O God, when I encounter the two impostors
    'triumph' and 'disaster,'
show me the truth once more.
Give me the good sense
to be neither puffed up with pride
nor plunged into gloom.
Pick me up and put me firmly
on the narrow way that leads to freedom,
and redeem both my mistakes and my successes
in your abundant mercy.

> Rudyard Kipling (1865–1936) spoke of 'Triumph' and
> 'Disaster' equally as 'impostors', in his poem 'If –'.

38

Forgive us, Lord,
when we want proofs for our faith,
and demand absolute certainty
before we will commit ourselves to you.
Strengthen our trust in you,
so that we, who have not seen you,
may still believe;
and in believing may be blessed
with the fullness of joy,
now and always.

Thomas and the risen Jesus, John 20:24–29

39

O Christ, our Morning Star,
Splendour of Light Eternal,
shining with the glory of the rainbow,
come and waken us
from the greyness of our apathy
and renew in us your gift of hope.

The Venerable Bede (671–735)

40

We grieve and confess
that we hurt and have been hurt,
to the third and fourth generations,
that we are so afraid of pain
that we shield ourselves from being vulnerable to
    others,
and refuse to be open and trusting as a child . . .

O God of Wholeness, we rest in you . . .
You listen with us to the sound of running water,
you sit with us under the shade of the trees of our
    healing,
you walk once more with us in the garden in the
    cool of the day,
the oil of your anointing penetrates the cells of
    our being,
the warmth of your hands steadies us and gives us
    courage.
O God of wholeness, we rest in you.

Jim Cotter

LORD, GUIDE ME

41

Jesus my Teacher, guide me along your way, and help me to piece together the jigsaw of life in your kingdom. When I make decisions, lead me to the heart of the matter; and when I face conflict, do not let my own panic drown out the still, small voice of your wisdom.

42

Christ my Guide,
be with me on my pilgrimage through life:
    when I falter, encourage me,
    when I stumble, steady me,
    and when I have fallen, pick me up.

Help me to become, step by step, more truly
    myself,
and remind me that you have travelled this way
    before me.

43

When I want to run – hold me.
When I want to turn away – turn me round.
When I want to hide – race me to my hiding place
    and win.
When I want to hurt others – deflect my aim.
When I want to hurt myself – love me.
When I cry – grab me quickly
    and rock me safely
    in your strong arms.

Ruth Burgess

44

Stay at the centre of my soul, O God:
      be in my longing and my hurting;
      be in my hoping and my emptiness;
      be in my eyes and lips and heart,
so that my desire to be true to you
and to myself
may prevail over everything else.

45

Lord, guard my lips;
free me from
the clutter of unnecessary words,
the clamour of vengeful words,
and the cleverness of cynical words.
Teach me when to be silent,
and when silence would mean cowardice or
unkindness.
Let all my words be well used,
coming from a quiet point within me
where you are,
the Word,
at the heart of my life.

Psalm 141:3

46

O Lord, Jesus Christ,
    stay beside me to defend me,
    within me to guide me,
    before me to lead me,
    behind me to guard me,
    and above me to bless me;
that with you and in you
I may live and move and have my being,
for ever and ever.

Source unknown

47

Thank you, Lord, for the gift of the Scriptures.
As I reflect on the Bible,
make me open to your wisdom,
receptive to your will
and courageous in my response;
in the love of Jesus,
Rabbi, Teacher, Friend.

LORD, GIVE ME COURAGE

48

Lord, give me grace to follow the example of your
    saints,
in a spirit of joy and not of self-righteousness.
May my life be ruled,
not by fear of what anyone can do to me,
but by delight in your will,
trust in your presence,
and freedom in your service.

49

Jesus, where are you taking me?
    Into joy.
    Into pain.

I am afraid,
but to do anything other than go with you
would be to die inwardly;
and to look for wholeness apart from you
would be to lose my true self.
So I come to you,
protesting and confused,
but loving you all the same.
You will have to hold on to me
as we walk together
through this compelling and frightening landscape
of the kingdom of God.

50

When I feel threatened
or believe myself to be a failure,
give me courage to enter my still centre,
the place of buried treasure
and sunshine
and solitude
where you are, Lord,
and where it no longer matters
who approves of me

or how successful I am
because you are there,
and, in your presence,
I rediscover the confidence
to be me.

54

Sometimes I feel stuck and helpless,
    rigid with anxiety
    and unable to move on;
like the paralysed man, I rely on my friends to carry me
    and hold me before you, Lord.
I need your assurance
that I am accepted and forgiven.
Release me from all my fears,
and help me to trust you enough to stand up
and willingly take hold of
whatever you give me to carry.

Mark 2:1–12

52

I give thanks for the courage of the martyrs;
and I ask for strength to stand up for what I believe.

I give thanks for the courage of all who refuse to
    deny you;
and I ask for strength to stay firm when the crowd
    disagrees.

I give thanks for the generosity of your saints;
and I ask for delight in the gift of each moment.

Father of mercy,
bless my efforts to love you,
and help me, in spite of my uncertainties,
    to hear your call,
    follow your way,
and surrender my life into your hands.

FEAR OF DEMENTIA

53

If one day I should lose my mind,
Lord, let me still be yours,
even if I cease to understand
what being 'yours' may mean.
I fear the indignity of people saying, 'Poor soul,
she's not the person that she used to be.'
Lord, if this should happen,
let my condition be
an offering for the millions of others
who have faced inner confusion and the loss of self.
O God, even my fear of 'going mad'
is outstripped by your love
into eternity.

So help me to forget about tomorrow,
and concentrate on living in today.

FEAR OF DEATH

54

Gentle and mysterious God,
you gave me the gift of life,
and will be with me at my death;
I am afraid of dying suddenly, violently or painfully,
and I dread leaving behind those I love.
I give you my fears, as a gift of trust in you.
Help me to face the truth that we are all dying,
and let me remember
that if I can face up to my mortality with honesty,
I can live more fully now.

55

Jesus, remember me,
as you remembered the man who was dying next
    to you;
Jesus, remember me,
as you remember all who are lonely and frightened;
and, when I die, take me into your loving arms
and show me that your kingdom has never been
    far away.

56

Lord of eternity,
whose power is infinite,
whose days are without number
and whose mercy is beyond our fathoming,
keep my face turned always towards you,
so that, each day, I remember
that life is your gift,
and the hour of my death unknown.
And when finally I meet you face to face,
transform me in the fire of your love,
and receive me into your eternal kingdom.

LORD, USE ME

57

Lord, I give you my love;
accept it, as you accepted loaves and fishes from a
    young lad.
Use my small offering to bless many,
and make good the poverty of my efforts
by the richness of your bounty.

The feeding of the five thousand, Mark 6:35–44

58

Lord,
let my life be a space
in which you can work in the world.
Clear away my inner rubbish,

and fill me with your Spirit
of healing, delight and peace,
so that everything I do
may be the fruit of your life in me.

59

Lord, let the flame of your love
set on fire my whole heart.
May I wholly burn towards you,
wholly love you,
set aflame by you.

Saint Augustine of Hippo (354–430)

60

Abba, Father,
I am here,
for you,
for myself,
for the world,
for this moment,
I am here ...

61

Lord, let me be a channel of your blessing to
others. I do not know how you will use my
prayers, but I trust you absolutely, that I may
play my part in your healing and redeeming
work in the world.

62

Lord God, I am no longer my own, but yours.
Put me to what you will,
rank me with whom you will.
Put me to doing, put me to enduring;
let me be employed for you,
or laid aside for you,
exalted for you
or brought low for you;
let me be full, let me be empty;
let me have all things
let me have nothing.
I freely and wholeheartedly yield all things
to your pleasure and disposal.
And now, glorious and blessed God,

Father, Son and Holy Spirit,
you are mine and I am yours.
So be it.

John Wesley (1703–1791)

63

Lord of my life,
I give you my time,
my reputation,
my worries
and my desires.
Thank you
that you receive whatever I offer
and transform it,
so that this gift of my life
is taken up
into your great energy of love.

64

O living God,
draw all the fragments of my life
into the bright mosaic of your love;
weave all the tangled threads of my desires
into the tapestry you are spreading,
like a rainbow,
on the loom of the world;
and help me celebrate
the many facets
and the dazzling colours
of your peace.

Julie M. Hulme

65

O God, enlarge my heart
    that it may be big enough to receive the
    greatness of your love.
Stretch my heart
    that it may take into it all those who with me
    around the world
    believe in Jesus Christ.

Stretch it
    that it may take into it all those who do not
    know him,
    but who are my responsibility because I know
    him.
And stretch it
    that it may take in all those who are not lovely
    in my eyes,
    and whose hands I do not want to touch;
through Jesus Christ, my Saviour.

                    Prayer of an African Christian

66

O Christ, you lived and breathed everything that
    matters.
Whatever the Spirit that was in you,
    let it be in me as well.
Whatever the energy
    that healed those who came into contact with
    you,
    let it flow through me as well.
Fill me with the vision, the tenderness and the
    passion
    that filled you.

67

Lord, quieten me, as I place in your hands those
for whom I want to pray. I know that you love
them with a love greater than I could ever imagine.
In the stillness I am here, with you, for them. Use
me, Lord.

68

Abba, Father,
with you, in my sinfulness,
offering the world;
with you in my weariness,
offering the world;
with you in my need of you,
offering the world;
with you in unbounded trust,
offering the world.

69

Lord,
I cannot fathom or hold you;
I can only ask you
to take hold of me.
I cannot grasp or contain you
in a formula or tradition;
I can only ask you to fill me with yourself,
and make me part
of the mystery of your presence
in the world.

70

Lord,
you trust me,
you free me,
you love me,
you fill me,
you share your work with me,
you are my life.

71

If every part of my life
is with you
and in you, Lord,
then everything is made good:
even the things I struggle not to resent,
even the draining and hurtful encounters.
Let every moment of my life be your moment,
whether or not I consciously remember you,
and make me more open
to the pulse of your life
and the breath of your love.

72

Behold, Lord, an empty vessel that needs to be
filled. My Lord, fill it. I am weak in the faith;
strengthen me. I am cold in love; warm me and
make me fervent that my love may go out to my
neighbour. I do not have a strong and firm faith;
at times I doubt and am unable to trust you alto-
gether. O Lord, help me and strengthen my faith
and trust in you.

Martin Luther (1483–1546)

73

O Christ,
your call draws us but never ensnares us;
show us what it means
to leave self behind
and follow you all our days;
and teach us to trust you enough
to give you everything
as raw material for your work
of healing and reconciliation in the world,
for your love's sake.

74

Lord Jesus Christ,
fill us, we pray, with your light
that we may reflect your wondrous glory.
So fill us with your love
that we may count nothing too small to do for you,
nothing too much to give,
and nothing too hard to bear.

Saint Ignatius Loyola (1491–1556)

75

Lord, you entered into the world and became
flesh so that the love which abides with the world
could still be seen and felt. By your grace, enable
us to enter into your healing life with loving and
caring action, as your Spirit shall lead.

CARA

76

Use us now as channels of blessing for those in
    need:
for victims of famine, especially in . . . ,
for victims of war, especially in . . . ,
for victims of hatred, prejudice and injustice,
for those who are ill or depressed, lonely or long-
    ing to be alone,
for those who have lost all hope of finding a
    home, or work.
Risen Christ,
breaking the bonds of evil and death,
shine on us, and on those for whom we pray,
with your compassion and glory.

Let your light flood the darkness in us and in our
    world,
and make us bearers of
    your healing for people,
    your delight in this planet,
    and your outrageously generous forgiveness,
on which we all depend,
through Christ, our Lord, our Lover and our
    Saviour. Amen.

LORD, HELP ME TO BE STILL

77

In the silence
I receive once more
this gift of my life
from you.
> Hold me in your stillness,
> simplify me,
> and take possession of me,
> my God.

78

Lord,
this moment is yours;
mine for you,
and yours for me.

I need you,
I cannot survive without you;
and yet I go on rushing through life
as if I could do everything in my own strength.
Forgive me.
I know
that you care for me at all times,
and that I am always in your hands;
but I still need to pause
and let my heart and spirit
be loved by you
into loving you again.

79

O Father, give my spirit power to climb
To the fountain of all light, and be purified.
Break through the mists of earth, the weight of
    clay,
Shine forth in splendour, you who are calm
    weather,
And quiet resting-place for faithful souls.
    You carry us, and you go before;
    You are the journey, and the journey's end.

Boethius (c. 480–524)

80

Lord, teach me the silence of love, the silence of
wisdom, the silence of humility, the silence of
faith, the silence that speaks without words.

O Saviour, teach me to silence my heart that I may
listen to the gentle movement of the Holy Spirit
within me, and sense the depths which are God,
today and always.

Frankfurt, 16th century

81

Make me
    a still place of light
    a still place of love
    of you
    your light radiating
    your love vibrating
    your touch and your healing
    far flung and near
    to the myriads caught
    in darkness, in sickness
    in lostness, in fear

make a heart-centre here
Light of the world.

Malling Abbey

82

Lord, make us people of stillness.

Help us to be empty before you,
that we may be filled with your peace;

teach us to be quiet in your presence,
that we may listen to your words;

and give us confidence to expose our whole being
    to you,
and meet you in the silence.

THANK YOU, LORD

83

My Father, you have carried me through all my
      wanderings
      and loved me through my rebelliousness.
I praise you.
You have given me untold riches:
      friends to love,
      beauty to enjoy,
      quiet spaces.
I praise you for life on this planet,
      for trust between people,
      and the unimaginable gift of the gospel.
Keep me thankful all my days,
that, against all the odds,
I may never lose sight
of hope and delight.

84

Thanks be to thee, my Lord Jesus Christ,
 for all the benefits thou hast won for me,
 for all the pains and insults thou hast borne
 for me.
O most merciful Redeemer, Friend and Brother,
 may I know thee more clearly,
 love thee more dearly,
 and follow thee more nearly,
 day by day.

Saint Richard of Chichester (1197–1253)

85

How can I tell of such love to me? You made me in
 your image and hold me in the palm of your
hand, your cords of love, strong and fragile as silk
 bind me and hold me.
 Rich cords, to family and friends,
 music and laughter echoing in memories,
 light dancing on the water, hills rejoicing.
Cords that found me hiding behind carefully built
 walls and led me out,

love that heard my heart break and despair and
rescued me,
love that overcame my fears and doubts and
released me.
The questions and burdens I carry you take,
to leave my hands free – to hold yours, and others,
free to follow your cords as they move and swirl in
the breeze,
free to be caught up in the dance of your love,
finding myself in surrendering to you.
How can I tell of such love? How can I give to such
love?
I am, here am I.

Catherine Hooper

86

Blessing and honour, thanksgiving and praise,
more than I can utter, more than I can understand, be yours, O most glorious Trinity, Father,
Son and Holy Spirit, by all angels, all people, all
creatures, now and for ever.

Lancelot Andrewes (1555–1626)

CREATION

87

God of delight, Source of all joy,
thank you for making me part of the web of life,
depending on the rhythms and fruits of the earth
for my existence.
Help me to be wholly present to you,
now, in this place,
where my feet are on the ground,
and where I am surrounded by creation's gifts,
from concrete to clouds,
if I have the wit to notice them!

88

For the earth in all its richness,
Praise to you, O Lord.

For rocks, mountains and islands, signs of your
strength and power,
Praise to you, O Lord.
For fossils, shells, and tiny creatures, single-cell
organisms and complex crustaceans, signs of
the continuity of your creation,

Praise to you, O Lord.
For fruits and nuts, berries, beans and blossoms,
    signs of your bounty,
Praise to you, O Lord.
For wind and clouds, stars and galaxies, signs of
    your infinite mystery,
Praise to you, O Lord.
For birds and fish, reptiles and all animals that
    walk on land, signs that you trust us not to
    abuse earth's creatures,
Praise to you, O Lord.
For varieties of language and differences in cultures,
    signs of the wealth of gifts that we share,
Praise to you, O Lord.
For similarities between peoples and our dependence
    on each other, signs that we are all made in your
    image,
Praise to you, O Lord.

Give us generous eyes and open hands, Creator
    God, whom we praise with all our heart.

MUSIC

89

Thank you, Lord, for music:
for rich harmonies and compelling rhythms;
for peaceful melodies and the great, stirring
   choruses.
When I listen to music,
or share in making it,
help me to do so with my full attention,
so that my heart as well as my head
may appreciate the hints of glory that music
   can give.

HOLIDAYS

90

Thank you, Father, for the rhythm of rest and
Sabbath at the heart of creation. Bless those who
are on holiday now; may they be refreshed and
recreated, and come home with new vision,
energy and contentment.

A PLACE OF PILGRIMAGE

94

Thank you, Father, for this ancient place of prayer:
  for the faith that has blossomed here,
  and for worship in all seasons offered here;
  for the lives that have been touched here,
  and commitment stirred into life here.
As we tread in the footsteps of our mothers and
  fathers in the faith,
bless us and all who come here,
and speak to us with the whisper of your love;
for you are a God of renewal and steadfastness,
now and for ever.

Intercessions

For Those in Sickness or Distress

92

Jesus our Healer,
I commend to your gentle hands those who are
    sick ...
Ease their pain,
and heal the damage done to them
in body, mind or spirit.
Be present to them through the support of friends
and in the care of doctors and nurses,
and fill them with the warmth of your love
now and always.

93

Lord Jesus, when you walked among hurt and
    lonely people,
you looked at them with understanding
and approached them with arms outstretched,
showing them that they were truly loved.
Come, now, and touch all who are in pain and
    distress ...
Heal those who have stopped believing in them-
    selves,
comfort those who are at the end of their tether,
and pour into their hearts the gentle balm of your
    Spirit.

PRAYERS TO ACCOMPANY
THE LAYING-ON OF HANDS

94

In the name of Jesus Christ, may the healing
power of the Holy Spirit make you whole, and
keep you entire, working in you according to
his most loving will.

Dorothy Kerin (1889–1963) (adapted)

95

May the light of God surround you,
the presence of God enfold you,
and the power of God heal you,
now and always.

for other blessings see Nos. 142 and 148

FOR THOSE AFFECTED BY HIV AND AIDS

96

Lord Jesus, you reached out to touch the leper and the outcast: reach out in love to those with HIV and AIDS, and those who love them. Give courage to their doctors, nurses and friends, so that their touch may be a channel for your healing and strengthening grace.

Lord Jesus, you were brought to the cross by hostility and prejudice: open our eyes to the challenge of HIV and AIDS. Make us ready to learn before we speak; may our words dispel hatred and build up compassion; and may we serve your spirit of truth and your kingdom of goodness.

Newcastle Churches' AIDS Awareness

FOR THE MENTALLY ILL

97

Father, we pray for the mentally ill, for all who are of a disturbed and troubled mind. Be to them light in their darkness, their refuge and strength in time of fear. Give special skills and tender hearts to all who care for them, and show them how best to assist in your work of healing; through Jesus Christ our Lord.

Timothy Dudley-Smith

FOR THE LONELY

98

Lord, I pray for all who are lonely:
children who are being bullied and dare not tell
    anyone;
shy people who find it hard to make friends;
those who feel rejected and isolated;
those whose partner has died or left them;
and elderly people who miss their families and old
    friends.
Lord, be with them all, in your infinite love.

For the dying

99

Lord, I pray for those
whose life on earth is almost at an end,
especially for this your beloved child *N.;*
may *he* be filled with your peace,
and surrender *himself* totally into your hands,
knowing that you have loved *him*
with an everlasting love.

At a miscarriage, a still birth, or the death of a new-born baby

100

O God, in whose hands are both life and death,
be with us as we struggle to understand
the dying of this tiny child.
We entrust that life into your care.
Comfort *N.* on this day of grief, and in the weeks
    that lie ahead;
in the love of Jesus Christ our Lord.

FOR SOMEONE WHO HAS DIED

101

We commend into your hands, O Lord, those
    whom we have loved,
especially *N.*
You gave *her* breath,
and loved *her* through *her* life.
Receive *her* now in your infinite tenderness,
and give *her* peace.

FOR THE BEREAVED

102

Lord Jesus Christ, you wept at the death of
Lazarus whom you loved; bless and comfort
our friends in their loss. Give them courage
and companionship as they adjust to their new
situation, and be with them as they grieve.

FOR OUR HOMES, FAMILIES AND FRIENDS

103

O Lord, bless our household;
grant us health and peacefulness,
fun and friendship,
and a warm and welcoming spirit.
Bless the working, the relaxing,
the loving and the sharing
that will happen here;
and may the Spirit of Christ rest on us
now and always.

104

Lord, help us to listen to each other,
    to be gentle with one another,
    to forgive each other
    and to be willing to laugh at ourselves.

COMMITMENT

105

God of love and trust,
bless our hopes, our risk-taking and our
    commitment;
make us sensitive and forgiving,
and give us the wisdom
to allow each other freedom and space.
Let our love be for the world around us
as well as for each other,
and keep us centred on you.

FOR A WOMAN WHO WILL SOON GIVE BIRTH

106

God of love,
bless our friend who will soon be giving birth;
hold her in the pain,
strengthen her in the weariness,
breathe in her,
labour in her,
and bring forth through her this child
whom we await with loving anticipation.

A NEW-BORN BABY

107

We praise you, Lord, for this most precious gift of
    a child;
may God the Father guard *him,*
may God the Son guide *him,*
may God the Holy Spirit fill *him*
with gentleness and peace
all the days of *his* life.

AN ADOPTED CHILD

108

Lord, thank you that *N.* has been chosen to be
    part of *N.* and *N.*'s family.
Bless *her,* and *her* new parents.
May they grow together in love, laughter, learning
    and sharing,
so that the world may be enriched
by their openness to others,
and their delight in living.

A PARENT'S PRAYER

109

Lord, I offer my daily life with my children
as a prayer
for all children of the world,
especially those who are
unloved,
abused,
starving,

bullied,
orphaned,
or afraid.

I offer my struggle with the demands of parent-
    hood as a prayer
for other parents,
those who face similar difficulties,
and those whose problems are different.

I offer my enjoyment of my children
    as a prayer
for childless couples,
bereaved parents,
single parents who ache for someone to share
    the load,
adopted children who have been told the truth
    too late,
women who have had abortions,
aborted babies,
and for all the secure and contented children too.

CHILDREN

110

O God, we place our children in your hands.
We ask
not that you will shield them from difficulty,
> but that you will give them the strength to
> face it;
not that you will protect them from making mistakes,
> but that they may be able to learn from them;
not that their lives will be easy,
> but that they will deal with its challenges
> courageously.
Be with them when they are vulnerable,
protect them from lasting harm,
and keep them always in your love.

Teenagers

111

Lord God,
help us to learn from our teenagers
how best to accompany them
through these turbulent years.
Make us sensitive and patient,
and give us the wisdom to support them
in our challenging and confusing world.
May they grow in understanding
of what matters most in life,
so that they become generous, strong and
    thoughtful adults;
through Christ our Lord.

112

Lord, when our children have different tastes and
    ideas from our own,
        show us when not to speak.
When they disagree with us over what we allow
    them to do,
        give us the wisdom to be neither over-protec-
        tive nor irresponsible.

And when they move away from us,
    help us to welcome their freedom,
    and to be always there for them when they
    need us.

113

Lord, we pray for our young people as they leave
home for the first time. Help them to settle into
their new surroundings, and be with them as they
make friends and adjust to different patterns of
living. Watch over them, Lord, and guard them.

DURING SEPARATION

114

O God,
protect those whom we love and who are sepa-
    rated from us.
Guide them when they are uncertain,
comfort them when they are lonely or afraid,
and bless them with the warmth of your presence.

Thank you that neither space nor time
can cut us off from the love we have in each other
    and in you.

THE ELDERLY

115

We thank you, Lord, for the privilege of knowing
    elderly people:
thank you for their experience and wisdom,
and the stories they can tell us;
help us to understand if they feel lonely or frustrated,
and surround them with your peace,
so that they may be aware how very close you are.

FOR OUR
COMMUNITIES

116

O God of love, we ask you to give us love:
Love in our thinking, love in our speaking,
Love in our doing,
And love in the hidden places of our souls;
Love of our neighbours near and far;
Love of our friends, old and new;
Love of those with whom we find it hard to bear,
And love of those who find it hard to bear with us;
Love of those with whom we work,
And love of those with whom we take our ease;
That so at length we may be worthy to dwell
    with you,
Who are eternal love.

William Temple (1881–1944)

Racial harmony

117

God of peace,
we pray for a spirit of mutual interest and concern
between men and women of different colours, cul-
    tures and creeds.
Touch the wounds that racism has inflicted,
heal those who have suffered verbal or physical
    abuse,
and make whole the people who inflicted those
    hurts.
Teach us to enjoy our diversity
and help us to move, always in hope,
towards a truly peaceful community of peoples.

118

Across the barriers that divide race from race:
    reconcile us, O Christ, by your cross.
Across the barriers that divide the rich from the poor:
    reconcile us, O Christ, by your cross.

Across the barriers that divide people of different
  faiths:
    reconcile us, O Christ, by your cross.
Across the barriers that divide Christians:
    reconcile us, O Christ, by your cross.
Across the barriers that divide men and women,
  young and old:
    reconcile us, O Christ, by your cross.

From a Madrid Basic Christian Community (adapted)

PLACES OF EDUCATION

119

O God, we pray for our schools and universities,
  (especially . . .).
Help us to value the experience of studying for its
  own sake.
Bless our life together as a learning and teaching
  community,
and make us wise but not cunning,
    perceptive but not cynical,
    and generous in a world where greed and
    ruthlessness often prevail;
in the name of Jesus Christ our Lord.

SCIENCE AND TECHNOLOGY

120

God of energy and power,
in the risk of creation
you have entrusted to us
a vast and dangerous knowledge of your world.
Give us wisdom and integrity
to use the skills of science
and the resources of technology
for the needs of the poor and forgotten,
and for the enriching and healing of us all.

FOR A SHOP, OFFICE, FACTORY OR OTHER PLACE OF WORK

121

God of creation,
bless all who work in this building,
and those who come to use it [*or* buy in it].
May it be a place
of care and honesty,

justice and kindness,
so that all who enter it
may glimpse something of your kingdom.

UNEMPLOYMENT

122

Thank you for our country, Lord. Thank you for the talents of each person living here. Forgive us when we allow people to count for nothing, when we cannot share our resources fairly, and when we want more for ourselves, although our neighbour has less. Be with those who, at the height of their powers, have been deprived of their jobs, and give hope to those who have never known the prospect of employment; through Jesus Christ, our Lord.

Church Action with the Unemployed (adapted)

For the Healing
of the Nations

123

O God,
Creator of our diverse humanity,
we thank you that you are found and worshipped
in every land,
in dance and community,
in suffering and peace-making,
in silence and singing and the faithfulness of your
people.
Forgive us when we tie our own hands
through prejudice or an ungenerous spirit;
and lead us, together,
to value our many traditions
and to listen to the wisdom that we can offer each
other.

124

God of revelation,
whose mercy embraces all peoples and nations:
tear down the walls which divide us,
break open the prisons which hold us captive
and so free us to celebrate your beauty
in all the earth;
through Jesus, our Brother and Redeemer.

Celebrating Common Prayer

125

O Lord Jesus,
stretch forth your wounded hands in blessing over
    your people,
to heal and to restore,
and to draw them to yourself and to one another
    in love.

Prayer from the Middle East

126

Show us, good Lord,
the peace we should seek,
the peace we must give,
the peace we can keep,
the peace we must forgo,
and the peace you have given
in Jesus Christ our Lord.

Caryl Micklem,
used by the Corrymeela Community, N. Ireland

127

Lord, as we remember with sadness the horror of
    war,
help us to work for a better understanding
between races and nations.
Open our eyes to see our own part
in discord and aggression between people now;
forgive us our pride and divisions,
and renew in us the search for peace,
so that trust may replace suspicion,
friendship replace fear,
and your spirit of reconciliation be known
    among us.

FOR VICTIMS OF VIOLENCE OR NATURAL DISASTERS

128

We pray
for all who have been maimed or murdered,
and those who were traumatized through watch-
    ing the brutality of others.
We pray
for people buried under bombed-out buildings,
and the victims of earthquakes, fires and mining
    accidents.
We pray
for those with smoke in their nostrils and dust in
    their mouths,
lost and, perhaps, unremembered.
Lord, in your tenderness, hold them.

PRISONERS OF CONSCIENCE

129

Lord, we pray for our brothers and sisters
who are in prison because of their stand against
    injustice,
and for all the other people who have 'disappeared'.
We pray for those undergoing torture;
Lord, give them strength, and the sense that they
    are not alone.
In particular we hold before you
those who believe that the world has forgotten
    them.
May they know that there are people who care,
and who are praying for them.
Jesus, arrested and tortured yourself,
be with them now.

THE HUNGRY AND THE POOR

130

O God, who created us out of love, we pray for
all who are destitute and without hope. Help us to
understand what it is like to be poor or marginal-
ized, to have no clean water, or to be exhausted
by the sheer struggle to survive. Fire our imagina-
tion, and empower us to work for the relief of
their suffering; through Jesus Christ our Lord.

131

Lord, heal your Church:
heal the wounds of the past,
and those we inflict on each other now.
Free us from party-spirit,
and lift up our hearts to you,
so that we may be filled
with resurrection joy beyond all division,
and with your spirit of love
which nothing can destroy.

132

Gracious Father, we pray for your church.
Fill it with your truth, and keep it in your peace.
Where it is corrupt, purge it;
where it is in error, direct it;
where it is right, strengthen and confirm it;
where it needs help, provide for it;
where it is divided, heal it,
and unite it in your love, through Jesus Christ our
    Saviour.

After William Laud (1573–1645)

133

God our healer,
whose mercy is like a refining fire:
touch us with your judgement,
and confront us with your tenderness;
that, being comforted by you,
we may reach out to a troubled world,
through Jesus Christ.

Janet Morley

134

Lord Jesus, killed by hate and raised by love,
help us to be Your witnesses in a hostile world,
to show most love where there is most hate,
and to live united with one another until You
    come again.

Susan Williams

135

Healing God,
we thank you for Saint Luke,
Paul's 'beloved physician',
and for his faithful recording
of the life of your Son
and the birth of the church.
Continue in us your work of healing:
may we never pass by on the other side,
but rather reach out to the poor and sick
and those on the margins,
in the love of Jesus our Lord.

Colossians 4:14

136

All-loving Christ,
we pray for those who have lost their faith,
and all who are questioning and searching.
Make us sensitive in listening to them,
and keep us from being judgemental or inward-
    looking.
We pray, too, for those who have recently found
    new faith;
may we in the church accompany them with
    warmth and wisdom,
so that, together, we may grow into a deeper
    knowledge of you,
for your love's sake.

137

Lord, we pray for the unity of your church.
Help us to see ourselves as rays from the one sun,
branches of a single tree,
and streams flowing from one river.

May we remain united to you and to each other,
because you are our common source of life;
and may we send out your light
and pour forth your flowing streams over all the
    earth,
drawing our inspiration and joy from you.

After Saint Cyprian of Carthage (c. 200–258)

Day's Beginning,
Day's Ending

IN THE MORNING

138

Each morning, Lord, I hold out my life to you,
an empty vessel for you to fill.
I give back to you this gift of a new day.
In your mercy,
redeem today's mistakes
and rescue its good intentions,
so that what I am
may reflect your life in me.

139

I arise today
through God's mighty strength,
his power to uphold me,

his wisdom to guide me,
and his hand to guard me.
I arise today,
through Christ's mighty strength,
through his death and resurrection,
through the Spirit's empowering,
through the presence of angels
and the love of the saints,
through the threefold Trinity
to protect me from evil.

Saint Patrick (c. 389–c. 461)

140

This day, Lord, may I dream your dreams;
this day, Lord, may I reflect your love;
this day, Lord, may I do your work;
this day, Lord, may I taste your peace.

141

O secret Christ,
Lord of the rose of dawn,
hide me
within thy silent peace,
that, throughout the turmoil of the day,
I may abide within the quiet of the daybreak.

Used in the chapel at Launde Abbey (source unknown)

142

May the warmth of Christ fill you
    the eyes of Christ gaze on you,
    and the peace of Christ shine through you,
    for the blessing of you and all whom you meet
    today and evermore.

In the Evening

143

May the song of your Spirit soothe me,
your gentle arms cradle me,
your tenderness ease my tiredness
and your welcome enfold my weariness,
this night and all my nights.

144

Jesus,
you sometimes spent whole nights alone in
prayer:
be with me tonight if I cannot sleep.
Calm me in the dark silence,
and fill me with the peace of your presence
in the depth of the night-time quietness.

145

Watch, dear Lord, with those who wake or weep
tonight, and let your angels protect those who
sleep. Tend the sick. Refresh the weary. Sustain
the dying. Calm the suffering. Pity the distressed.
We ask this for your love's sake.

Saint Augustine of Hippo (354–430)

146

Visit, Lord, we pray, this place,
and drive far from it all the snares of the
enemy.
Let your holy angels dwell here to keep us in
peace,
and may your blessing be upon us evermore;
through Jesus Christ our Lord.

The Office of Compline

147

O Lord, support us all the day long of this troublous life, until the shadows lengthen, and the evening comes, and the busy world is hushed, and the fever of life is over, and our work is done.

Then, in your mercy, give us safe lodging, a holy rest, and peace at the last, through Jesus Christ our Lord.

John H. Newman (1801–1890)

148

Peace of the running waves to you,
Deep peace of the flowing air to you,
Deep peace of the quiet earth to you,
Deep peace of the shining stars to you,
Deep peace of the shades of night to you,
Moon and stars always giving light to you,
Deep peace of Christ, the Son of Peace, to you.

Traditional Gaelic blessing

Notes and Acknowledgements

3   Based on, 'He meets you in Gentleness' on page 46 of *Surprised by Light,* by Ulrich Schaffer, HarperCollins*Publishers* (1980).

14   Copyright © Ralph Wright, O.S.B., St Louis Abbey, 500 South Marston Road, Saint Louis, Missouri 63141–8500. Used with permission.

27   From *All Desires Known,* SPCK (1992). Used with permission.

31   Inspired by the 14th century invocation of Christ, 'Anima Christi'.

40   From *Prayer at Night,* Cairns Publications, 47, Firth Park Avenue, Sheffield S5 6HF. Used with permission.

64   Julie M. Hulme, The Bethany Project. Used with permission.

65   From *With All God's People,* World Council of Churches, Geneva (1990). Used with permission.

75   From CARA, Care and Resources for people
        affected by HIV/AIDS. Used with permission.

94   From *An Order of Service for the Laying-on of
        Hands,* used at Burrswood, Tunbridge Wells, a
        Christian centre for medical and spiritual care.

97   Timothy Dudley Smith, *New Every Morning*
        (1973).

118   From *Jesus Christ, the Life of the World: A
        Worship Book,* © World Council of Churches.
        Based on an original prayer, 'The Ministry of
        Reconciliation', in *Worship Now,* compiled by
        David Cairns et al., Saint Andrew Press,
        Edinburgh (1972).

124   Material from *Celebrating Common Prayer*
        (Mowbray), © The Society of St Francis 1992,
        is used with permission.

125   From *Morning, Noon and Night,* edited by
        John Carden, Highway Press/CMS (1976).
        Used with permission.

133   From *All Desires Known,* SPCK (1992). Used
        with permission.

134   From *Lord of our World,* Falcon Press (1973).
        Falcon Books were published by CPAS, who
        are now at Athena Drive, Tachbrook Park,
        Warwick, CV34 6NG. Used with permission.

INDEX OF SUBJECTS